Make it Easy

Age 9-10

English

GW00400013

Contents

Alison Head and Louis Fidge

Nouns

A **noun** names a thing or a feeling.

Common nouns name a person or thing.

Abstract nouns name a feeling or idea.

sheep   man

love   anger

 Sort the words in the box into common nouns and abstract nouns.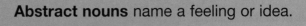

Common nouns	Abstract nouns
_____	_____
_____	_____
_____	_____
_____	_____
_____	_____
_____	_____
_____	

hatred coat
fear darkness
night lion
jealousy school
height
knowledge
house bus
expertise joy

 Look at each abstract noun. Then write a sentence that includes it.

a sympathy _____

b hope _____

c gratitude _____

d strength _____

e despair _____

f depth _____

g courage _____

h comfort _____

Plurals

Plural means **two or more** of something.

Most plurals end in s.	Words ending s, x, sh, or ch usually end es.	Words ending with a consonant followed by y end ies.
 cat**s**	 fox**es**	 bab**ies**

I Underline the correctly spelt word in each group.

a patchs   patchies   patches

b toys   toyes   toyies

c worrys   worries   worryes

d trys   tryes   tries

e penes   pennes   pens

f dishes   dishs   dishies

g citys   cityes   cities

h caks   cakes   cakies

II Write down the plurals of these words.

a hat   _____

b party   _____

c bush   _____

d box   _____

e lorry   _____

f bus   _____

g tree   _____

h cry   _____

i book   _____

j puppy   _____

Vowel endings

Most words that end with a vowel end in *e*, but some words end in *a*, *i*, *o* or *u*.

banana

spaghetti

domino

emu

Most of these words end in *s* in the plural and some, like *spaghetti*, are the same in the singular and in the plural. But some words that end in *o* end in *es* in the plural, like *buffaloes* and *dominoes*.

 Choose *a, i, o* or *u* to complete these words.

a past____

b cobr____

c pian____

d chapatt____

e gn____

f cell____

g tub____

h viol____

i risott____

j em____

k pizz____

l zebr____

m camer____

n are____

a   i   o   u

II Write the plural of these words. You will need to decide whether each one should end in *s* or *es*.

a zoo _____

b radio _____

c echo _____

d solo _____

e kimono _____

f hero _____

g domino _____

h disco _____

i yo yo _____

j cuckoo _____

Verbs

Verbs describe actions. Some verbs are active and some are passive.

Robbie **blew** out the candle.

This verb is **active**. It describes what Robbie does.

Robbie **was blown** over by the wind.

This verb is **passive**. It explains what happens to Robbie.

I Underline the verb in each sentence. Then tick the box to say whether you think it is active or passive.

	active verb	passive verb
a Katie fell over.	☐	☐
b Ben ate the chips.	☐	☐
c The window was broken when the ball hit it.	☐	☐
d Mia picked a flower.	☐	☐
e The winning story was written by Jake.	☐	☐
f Mum drove me to school.	☐	☐
g Our house was built three years ago.	☐	☐
h The letter was delivered by the postman.	☐	☐
i We ran home quickly.	☐	☐
j The door was slammed by John.	☐	☐

II Write sentences using these verbs.

a played _____

b was played _____

c found _____

d be found _____

e saw _____

f were seen _____

g bought _____

h was bought _____

Nouns and verbs

All sentences contain a noun or pronoun and a verb.

If the noun is **singular**, you must use the singular verb form.

If the noun is **plural**, you must use the plural form of the verb.

singular noun   singular verb form

The <u>cat</u> **plays** with the ball.

plural noun   plural verb form

The <u>cats</u> **play** with the ball.

I   Choose the correct verb form from the words in bold to match each noun.

a The girls _____ netball.   **plays**   **play**

b The rabbits _____ the grass.   **nibble**   **nibbles**

c She _____ every day.   **swims**   **swim**

d The children _____ the sweets.   **gobbles**   **gobble**

e The birds _____ away.   **fly**   **flies**

f Apples _____ on trees.   **grows**   **grow**

g We _____ late.   **are**   **am**

h My bike _____ mending.   **needs**   **need**

II   Choose a verb from the box to complete each sentence. Make sure you use the correct form of the verb you choose.

a The dog _____ its tail.

b Postmen _____ letters.

c A cow _____ grass.

d In winter it _____ very cold.

e Pandas _____ bamboo.

f Santa Claus _____ presents.

g Cats _____ mice.

h Weekends _____ great!

chase

delivers

eat

are

eats

deliver

chases

is

Commas in complex sentences

Complex sentences contain more than one clause. Commas help to separate these clauses.

After breakfast, we went to school.

The subordinate clause gives us extra information.

The main clause gives us the key information.

I **Underline the main clause in each sentence.**

a It was hot, so we had a cold drink.

b My birthday is in October, just before Hallowe'en.

c On Friday, we are going on holiday.

d Because it was so dark, we took a torch.

e We flew to Greece, on an aeroplane.

f Susie is my best friend, although I haven't known her very long.

g The window got broken, but it was an accident.

h The shop was shut, so we couldn't buy any sweets.

II **Add commas to each sentence to separate the main and subordinate clauses. Then underline the main clause.**

a It was raining hard so I took an umbrella.

b The bus was late so we had to walk.

c Because it was Saturday we could play football all day.

d Max has chickenpox so he has to stay at home.

e I play the guitar although I'm not very good.

f Mum lost her keys so we had to call a locksmith.

g Dad drank all the tea so he had to buy some more.

h The television broke down so I read my book.

Word roots

Lots of the words we use come from other words.

approve

→ approval

→ disapprove

This can help us with spelling.

I **Write down two words from the box against each word root.**

> boring   relative   building   machinist   impress   lightning   breakfast
> operation   depression   rebuild   delight   breakable   cooperate
> machinery   relation   boredom

a bore _____ _____

b light _____ _____

c press _____ _____

d machine _____ _____

e break _____ _____

f operate _____ _____

g relate _____ _____

h build _____ _____

II **Write down two words that come from each of these root words.**

a act _____ _____

b take _____ _____

c electric _____ _____

d sign _____ _____

e claim _____ _____

f public _____ _____

g cover _____ _____

h child _____ _____

Spelling rules

Following spelling rules can help us to spell whole families of words. One useful rule helps us to add *full* to words. Another helps us to spell words containing a soft *c* sound.

When you use *full* as a suffix, the final *ll* becomes *l*.

When the letter *c* makes a soft sound, it is usually followed by *i*.

play**ful** beauti**ful** **ci**nnamon a**cci**dent

 Underline examples of the spelling rules above in these sentences.

a It was peaceful in the woods.

b I can't decide which book to read.

c I love living in a city.

d Gemma was careful when she crossed the road.

e The runners ran three circuits of the track.

f Kelvin was fearful he would be discovered.

g We are learning about decimals in maths.

h I am hopeful that I'll win the competition.

 Now use the spelling rules to find the incorrect spelling in each sentence. Underline the incorrect word, then write it correctly in the space.

a We saw a great film at the sinema. _____

b I love colourfull clothes. _____

c Some berries are harmfull if you eat them. _____

d There were clowns at the sircus. _____

e It is rude to speak with a mouthfull of cake. _____

f I made a difficult desision. _____

g The ballerina was very gracefull. _____

h We sat in a sircle. _____

Prefixes

We can add prefixes to the **beginning** of words to change their meaning.
Different prefixes have different meanings.

bi + plane = biplane

bi means two, so a biplane is a plane with two sets of wings.

I Complete these word sums.

a auto + graph = _____

b circum + ference = _____

c bi + focals = _____

d tele + photo = _____

e trans + parent = _____

f bi + lingual = _____

g circum + stance = _____

h trans + plant = _____

i auto + biography = _____

j tele + graph = _____

II Choose a prefix from the box to complete each word sum.

a <u>tele</u> + phone = <u>telephone</u>

b _____ + cycle = _____

c _____ + matic = _____

d _____ + late = _____

e _____ + lingual = _____

f _____ + mobile = _____

g _____ + vision = _____

h _____ + fer = _____

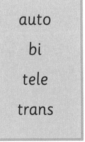

auto

bi

tele

trans

Synonyms

Synonyms are words that have similar meanings.

happy   joyful   excited   contented

Using synonyms can make your writing more interesting, but be careful to choose ones with exactly the right meaning.

I Choose the best synonym from the words in bold to complete each sentence.

a It was a _____ summer's day.   **hot   steaming**

b When my cup was _____ I asked for more juice.   **hollow   empty**

c Mr Fisher was _____ when I forgot my homework.   **angry   frustrated**

d The hedgehog is a _____ animal.   **ferocious   wild**

e Ranjit was _____ at the dentist.   **brave   heroic**

f I threw away my _____ toys.   **ancient   old**

g At the end of the race I was _____.   **exhausted   sleepy**

h I _____ the vase by mistake.   **broke   destroyed**

II Write a sentence using each of these synonyms.

a chilly   _____

b freezing   _____

c cold   _____

d icy   _____

e cool   _____

f frosty   _____

Idioms

We sometimes say things like:

'Jo opened a can of worms.'   or   'Alex and Kim are like two peas in a pod.'

We don't literally mean what we say. These phrases are called idioms.

 Draw lines to match up these common sayings (idioms) with their meanings.

a   out of order   happens very rarely

b   under the weather   just like a parent

c   peas in a pod   absolutely thrilled

d   over the moon   feeling unwell

e   worth her salt   a great person to have around

f   a chip off the old block   raining very hard

g   it's raining cats and dogs   very similar

h   once in a blue moon   not acceptable

 Write a sentence using each of these idioms.

a   right as rain

_____

b   sleeping like a log

_____

c   never in a month of Sundays

_____

d   paint the town red

_____

e   keep your eyes peeled

_____

f   down in the dumps

_____

Dialogue

When characters in a story **talk to each other**, we call it dialogue. When you write dialogue you need to follow rules, so your readers know who is saying what.

We put what our characters say in speech marks. We also start a new line when a different person speaks.

'I've lost my bike,' complained Martin.

'Where did you leave it?' asked Mrs Chaudri.

 Add the speech marks to this piece of dialogue.

a Do you want to come back to my house after school? asked Jamie.

b That would be great, replied Sasha. I'll have to check with my mum though.

c OK. If she says yes we could play with my new computer game.

d I'll go and ask her now, said Sasha. See you in a minute.

 Write this conversation as dialogue, including speech marks.

Dad: Have you done your homework?

John: Not all of it.

Dad: You'll have to do the rest after tea.

John: But I'm supposed to be playing football with Stephen.

Dad: Well, Stephen will just have to wait while you finish your homework.

_____

_____

_____

_____

_____

_____

_____

_____

_____

_____

Adverbs and dialogue

Dialogue is the name given to a conversation between characters in a story.

> Kelly said, 'It's my birthday soon.'
>
> 'Are you having a party?' replied Ashley.

Adverbs tell us **how** the characters talk, which can tell us a lot about how they are feeling.

> 'Yes, it's going to be great!' said Kelly, **excitedly**.

I   **Choose an adverb from the box to complete each sentence.**

a   'I won first prize!' said Mary _____.

b   'Excuse me,' whispered Phil _____.

c   'I want more!' demanded Owen _____.

d   'I'm sure I'll win,' said Ruby _____.

e   'I bet it will rain tomorrow,' complained Sam _____.

f   'You're late,' barked Mr Moor _____.

g   'I'm tired,' yawned Connor _____.

h   'It's not fair!' complained Ella _____.

gloomily

crossly

timidly

sleepily

confidently

rudely

proudly

sulkily

II   **Write sensible dialogue to complete this conversation. Look at the adverbs to give you clues about what Dad and Ben might be saying.**

a   '_____?' asked Dad patiently.

b   '_____,' replied Ben stubbornly.

c   '_____,' repeated Dad firmly.

d   '_____,' muttered Ben quietly.

e   '_____?' asked Dad angrily.

f   '_____,' replied Ben tearfully.

g   '_____,' said Dad wearily.

h   '_____,' sniffed Ben sulkily.

Writing plays

Plays tell stories, just like a book. A play script gives the actors performing the play the information they need to act out the story.

> [Beth's room, at night. Beth asleep in bed. A crash is heard off-stage]
>
> Beth [sitting up]: What was that?
>
> [Beth creeps to the door and listens. She is wearing pyjamas.] Sarah, are you awake?
>
> Sarah [sleepily]: No, I'm not!

The settings and costumes are described.

Stage directions tell the actors what to do and how to behave.

The dialogue tells them what to say.

Imagine you are writing a play script based on the following section of text. Write a description of the setting, and stage directions for Beth and Sarah.

> Beth crept to her sister's room. 'Sarah, wake up!' she whispered. Sarah rolled over and awoke slowly.
>
> 'What is it?' she grumbled.
>
> 'I can hear someone downstairs,' hissed Beth, creeping back to the door to listen.

Setting: _____

_____

Stage directions for Beth: _____

Stage directions for Sarah: _____

II **Decide what you think happens next in the story. Then write the next few lines of the play, including dialogue and stage directions.**

_____

_____

_____

_____

_____

_____

_____

Homophones

Homophones are words that sound the same, but are spelt differently and have different meanings.

knight

night

We need to be sure we pick the correct homophone to fit the sentence we are writing.

The **knight** rode bravely into battle.

As **night** fell, the moon came up.

I **Write down homophones for these words.**

a cereal _____

b allowed _____

c bored _____

d waist _____

e hymn _____

f beach _____

g steal _____

h tail _____

i leak _____

j week _____

II **Read this paragraph then circle the correct homophone from each pair in bold.**

We took our **fair fare** and went to **bye buy** a ticket for the boat trip. The **son sun** shone brightly as our boat docked at the **quay key**. A sailor with blonde **hair hare** **through threw** a long **peace piece** of rope to another sailor standing by us. He **tide tied** it in a huge **not knot** to secure the boat. When the **mane main** gangplank appeared, the passengers began to **board bored** the boat. We couldn't **weight wait** to set off!

Suffixes

We can add a suffix to the end of some words to change their meaning.

Lots of words end with suffixes that make a *shun* sound. Several suffixes make this sound.

physi**cian**	explo**sion**	se**ssion**	reduc**tion**
cian	sion	ssion	tion

I Choose *cian*, *sion*, *ssion* or *tion* to complete these word sums. Watch out for your spelling!

a politic + _____cian_____ = _____

b confuse + _____ = _____

c direct + _____ = _____

d discuss + _____ = _____

e educate + _____ = _____

f possess + _____ = _____

g optic + _____ = _____

h transfuse + _____ = _____

II Look carefully at the words in the box. Use them to help you decide which rule refers to each of the *shun* suffixes in the box. Then write down the correct suffix (*ssion*, *sion*, *cian*, *tion*) next to each rule.

Rules	Suffix
a Used where words end in **c**. Common in occupations.	_____
b Used where the base word ends in *d* or *de*; or *s* or *se*.	_____
c Makes a clear, soft *sh* sound.	_____
d Used where the other rules don't apply, making it the most common *shun* ending.	_____

magician

electrician

extension

explosion

passion

mission

fraction

reduction

fiction

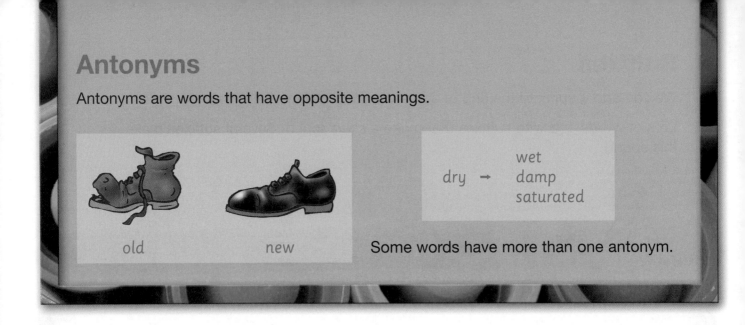

Antonyms

Antonyms are words that have opposite meanings.

old   new

dry → wet
        damp
        saturated

Some words have more than one antonym.

I Draw lines to join up the pairs of antonyms.

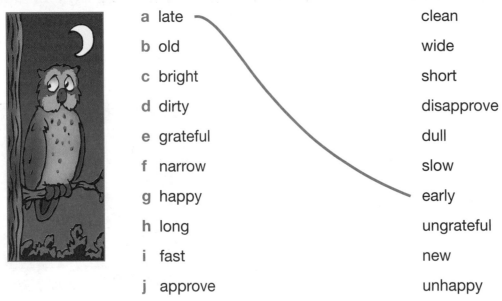

a late   clean
b old   wide
c bright   short
d dirty   disapprove
e grateful   dull
f narrow   slow
g happy   early
h long   ungrateful
i fast   new
j approve   unhappy

II Think of antonyms to fill the gaps in the story. Try not to use the same antonym twice.

Goldilocks found the bears' cottage in the woods and went inside. She tried the porridge. The **big** bear's porridge was too **hot**. The _____ bear's porridge was too _____. She sat down. The **big** bear's chair was too **high**. The _____ bear's chair was too _____. She tried their beds. The **big** bear's bed was too **hard**. The _____ bear's bed was too _____. Goldilocks fell **asleep**, but when the bears returned she was wide _____ immediately. The bears chased Goldilocks away. She ran **fast** and they were too _____ to catch her.

Onomatopoeia

Onomatopoeia means words that sound the same as the noises they describe.

hiss

hoot

They are very powerful describing words.

 Pick a word from the box to complete each sentence.

a The wind _____ in the trees.

b Dry leaves _____ underfoot.

c The piglet _____.

d The bell _____ to mark the hour.

e My chair fell over with a _____.

f The jelly _____ as I spooned it into my bowl.

g The tap _____.

h We _____ in the puddles.

> splashed
>
> dripped
>
> whispers
>
> crunch
>
> clanged
>
> squealed
>
> squelched
>
> crash

II **Write down what you think might be making these noises. Use the sound of the words to help you decide.**

a ping _____

b rip _____

c clatter _____

d shatter _____

e crunch _____

f rustle _____

g squeak _____

h fizz _____

Metaphorical expressions

A metaphor is where a writer describes something as if it were something else.

He was the black sheep of the family.

 Match up these metaphors with their meanings.

a She is a loose cannon.   She is a good person.

b She is a good egg.   We are treating ourselves.

c He is a closed book.   She can't be trusted.

d We have a skeleton in the cupboard.   She is unpredictable.

e We're pushing the boat out.   He is annoying.

f She is a wolf in sheep's clothing.   We have a family secret.

g He is a pain in the neck.   She is trustworthy.

h She is a safe pair of hands.   He is difficult to understand.

 Write down what you think each expression means.

a There's a bad apple in every barrel. _____

b He's a rock. _____

c Every cloud has a silver lining. _____

d She's a snake in the grass. _____

e He's like a bull in a china shop. _____

f You're an angel. _____

Personal pronouns

Pronouns take the place of a noun. They can save us from having to repeat the same noun again and again.

Personal pronouns replace proper nouns, like the names of people.

> Sam ate his crisps. **He** likes salt and vinegar flavour best.

They can also replace plural nouns that describe people or animals.

> **We** fed the rabbits. **They** love carrots.

I Underline the personal pronouns in these sentences.

a She has long hair.

b They were late.

c Mum brought us some drinks.

d We played football.

e Phone me later.

f I am ten years old.

g Are you going to the party?

h Tim watched them carefully.

II Write these sentences again, replacing the nouns in bold type with a personal pronoun.

a Susie is my friend and **Susie** lives next door.

_____

b The boys jumped on their bikes, because **the boys** didn't want to be late.

_____

c Sam and I bought some sweets and **Sam and I** had a bag each.

_____

d Jo and I went to the cinema and **Jo and I** bought some popcorn.

_____

e Mum and Dad left us with Gran last night, so **Mum and Dad** could go out.

_____

f Dad collects my sisters from school and then takes **my sisters** to Brownies.

_____

Subordinate clauses

A complex sentence has more than one clause. The main clause gives us the key information. The subordinate clause gives us extra information.

In some complex sentences, the subordinate clause is embedded in the sentence.

We use commas to separate the subordinate clause from the rest of the sentence.

The cat, **which was black**, ran up the tree.

subordinate clause

 Underline the embedded subordinate clause in each complex sentence.

a My friend, who is called Chris, is coming to tea.

b Tomorrow, after lunch, we are going to the zoo.

c My brother, who is older than me, is great at football.

d Yesterday, because it was hot, we went to the beach.

e Our teacher, Mrs Brooks, marked our books.

f The new cinema, in town, has five screens.

g Donuts, with holes in, are my favourite cakes.

 Write these pairs of sentences again as one sentence, using an embedded subordinate clause.

a My uncle is coming to visit. He is from Australia.

My uncle, who is from Australia, is coming to visit.

b Tomorrow we are going bowling. We will go after school.

_____

c The train was crowded. It was late.

_____

d The dog chased its tail. It is called Patch.

_____

e The new coat is really warm. It is blue.

_____

f Next week we are going on holiday. We are going on Tuesday.

_____

The narrator

When we read a story, we are reading the narrator's viewpoint.

Sometimes the narrator is one of the characters in the story.

I wish I could go to the ball.

Sometimes the narrator is not in the story at all.

Cinderella wished she could go to the ball.

I   **Read this story. Then tick the box to say who you think the narrator is.**

I used to be so worried. I had no money to buy food or new leather to make shoes to sell. One night I cut up the last piece of leather ready to sew the next morning and went to bed hungry. The next morning I awoke to find the finest pair of boots on the table. I sold the boots for a good price and bought more leather. That night the same thing happened again, and soon I was rich. One night I stayed awake and watched, and saw two tiny elves making the boots for me. I made them new clothes and boots to say thank you.

The narrator is not in the story. ☐

The narrator is the shoemaker. ☐

The narrator is one of the elves. ☐

II   **Rewrite the story of the elves and shoemaker from the point of view of a narrator, who is not a character in the story.**

_____

_____

_____

_____

_____

_____

_____

_____

_____

Words from other languages

We use lots of words that are borrowed from other languages.

pizza

Pizza is an Italian word.

bungalow

Bungalow is an Indian word.

I Look at the words in the box. Then list all the foods. Use a dictionary to help you.

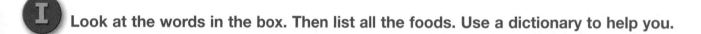

| macaroni mango sonata biryani risotto bongo chapatti tortilla tombola sauna chalet duvet chow mein gala moussaka cargo |

 _____   _____

_____   _____

_____   _____

_____   _____

II Choose which country in the box each word comes from. Then write a sentence for each word.

| Italy   India   Australia France   China |

a ballet _____

_____

b pasta _____

_____

c koala _____

_____

d wok _____

_____

e tandoori _____

_____

Word origins

Lots of the words we use started out as longer words.

Some words have letters missed out.	Some are used without their prefixes or suffixes.	Some are abbreviations or acronyms – they are made up from the initial letter of each word in a phrase.

of the clock → o'clock	telephone → phone	compact disc → CD

 Match up these words with their longer forms.

a Hallowe'en

b PC

c HGV

d pub

e salt 'n' vinegar

f plane

g HP

h bus

public house

salt and vinegar

aeroplane

hire purchase

omnibus

heavy goods vehicle

personal computer

all hallows' eve

 Write down the longer forms of these words.

a TV _____

b photo _____

c PE _____

d fish 'n' chips _____

e bike _____

f VIP _____

g MP _____

h fridge _____

i UK _____

Prepositions

Prepositions describe the relationship between two people or things.

The letters dropped **onto** the mat.

I brought the book **for** you.

I **Underline the prepositions in each sentence.**

a I kicked the ball over the fence.

b Dan peered through the window.

c Lily got a postcard from Amber.

d I went to Will's house after school.

e I found the missing shoe under my bed.

f Mark threw the rubbish into the bin.

g I sat between Jenny and Ellie.

h Jack hung his coat on a peg.

II **Write down a suitable preposition to complete each sentence.**

a We hid _____ the door.

b The bird flew _____ the house.

c Mum put a photo _____ the frame.

d The frog hopped _____ the pond.

e My teacher wrote _____ the whiteboard.

f The train rushed _____ the tunnel.

g We put a star _____ the Christmas tree.

h The cat walked _____ the wall.

Possessive apostrophes

Apostrophes can be used to show that something belongs to a person or thing.

Kate's house.

The men's cars.

The boy's bags.

The babies' toys.

With singular or collective nouns, the apostrophe goes before the *s*.

With plural nouns, the apostrophe goes after the *s*.

I Add the apostrophe to the nouns in these sentences.

a A dogs tail.

b The womens shopping.

c A girls books.

d Two boys socks.

e Four horses stables.

f The peoples cheers.

g A cooks apron.

h A cats kittens.

II Write these phrases again, making all the nouns plural and placing the apostrophe in the correct place.

a The cow's field.   *The cows' fields.* _____

b The teacher's pupil. _____

c The child's room.   _____

d The dog's kennel.   _____

e The hen's egg.   _____

f The baker's cake.   _____

g The man's shoe.   _____

h The car's tyre.   _____

Making notes

When we make notes, we only need to write down the key words. These key words will remind us later about other details.

Camels are specially adapted for desert living. They have soft, wide feet to help them walk in sand. Long eyelashes keep the sand out of their eyes. Their fatty humps store water.

camels

- adapted for desert
- wide feet
- long eyelashes
- fatty humps

 Look for the key words in this paragraph. Then write your own notes.

Dinosaurs have been extinct for millions of years. We know about them from fossils found in rocks. Some dinosaurs ate meat and some ate plants. Some lived on land, some could fly and some lived in the water.

_____

_____

_____

_____

_____

 Use this set of notes to write a paragraph about castles.

Castles

- defensive
- tall, thick walls
- built on hills – good view of enemy approach
- towers in walls – arrow slits

_____

_____

_____

_____

Possessive pronouns

We use possessive pronouns in the place of nouns to tell our readers that something belongs to a person or thing.

Kate picked up **her** coat.

The boys put on **their** boots.

When we use them, we must make sure we use the right form. Kate is a girl, so we use the singular female pronoun **her**.

There are lots of boys, so we use the plural pronoun **their**.

 Draw lines to match up the two halves of each sentence.

a The cat licked   his throne.

b Ben wrote to   their song.

c Sarah drank   its field.

d The king sat on   her juice.

e The bull charged across   our favourite film.

f The girls read   his pen pal.

g We watched   their books.

h They sang   its paws.

 Choose a possessive pronoun to complete these sentences.
Remember, the possessive pronoun its does not have an apostrophe!

a Sally visited _____ friend.

b They ate _____ packed lunches.

c Kieran finished _____ homework.

d We opened _____ presents.

e The spider scuttled across _____ web.

f I tidied _____ bedroom.

g They missed _____ bus.

h The bird flew to _____ nest.

Punctuation

Punctuation marks help our readers make sense of our writing.

,	•	!	?
Commas mark pauses in sentences, by separating clauses.	Full stops mark the end of sentences.	Exclamation marks can be used instead of full stops to show surprise, anger, joy or fear.	Question marks can also be used instead of full stops, to mark the end of a question.

I **Rewrite these sentences, putting the punctuation marks in the correct place.**

a After all, the hunting we found the key.

_____

b My favourite subject at school. is geography

_____

c It was great! on holiday

_____

d We tidied up then, got ready to go home.

_____

e What time? is it

_____

f Before, school we walked the dog.

_____

II **Add the punctuation and speech marks to this passage. The capital letters should give you some clues.**

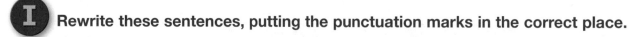

Last   September   we   moved   house   Our   new   house   is
brilliant   I   remember   when   Mum   said   we   were   going
to   move   Why   I   asked   She   said   Our   new   house
will   have   more   space   and   a   bigger   garden   She   was
right   Now   we   have   lots   of   space   and   my   best
friend   who   is   called   Julie   lives   next   door

Unstressed vowels

Many words with two or more syllables contain vowels that are difficult to hear when you say the word out loud. This can make the words tricky to spell.

literature

jewellery

I Underline the unstressed vowel in these words.

a general

b separate

c prosperous

d interested

e memorable

f offering

g difference

h library

i fastener

j desperate

k boundary

l conservatory

m generous

n history

o dangerous

p mystery

q boisterous

r christening

s listening

t stationery

II Correct the spelling of these words by writing them again, adding the unstressed vowel.

a frightning _____

b busness _____

c factry _____

d explanatry _____

e categry _____

f confrence _____

g refrence _____

h voluntry _____

i happning _____

j litracy _____

Test 1 Synonyms

Synonyms are words with **similar** meanings.

I feel **cold**.　　Yes, it is a bit **chilly**.

Match up the pairs of words with similar meanings.

1. help   tiny
2. sly   foe
3. small   gather
4. stop   aid
5. enemy   complain
6. moan   within
7. assemble   miserable
8. remedy   crafty
9. inside   ill
10. difficult   prevent
11. sick   wide
12. broad   crazy
13. quick   cure
14. sad   fast
15. mad   hard

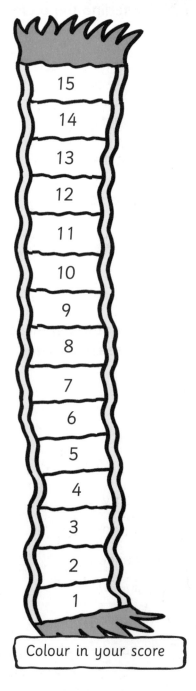

15
14
13
12
11
10
9
8
7
6
5
4
3
2
1

Colour in your score

32

Test 2 Direct and reported speech

We can write speech in two ways – as **direct speech** or **reported speech**.

The girl said, "My shoes are new."

This is **direct speech**. The girl's exact words are inside speech marks.

The girl said that her shoes were new.

This is **reported speech**. The girl's exact words are not used. Speech marks are not used either.

Write if each sentence uses direct or reported speech.

1. "I will dig the garden," Mr Jones said. _____

2. The man said that he didn't do it. _____

3. The boy shouted that he was hurt. _____

4. "My aunt is coming soon," Anna said. _____

5. She shouted, "Leave me alone!" _____

6. The lady asked if she could have some apples. _____

7. "Who lives here?" Ian asked. _____

8. Mark said that he was going on holiday. _____

9. The girl said that she wasn't ready yet. _____

10. "Be quiet," Emma whispered. _____

11. "The corn is ripe," the farmer said. _____

12. Sam boasted that he could climb the tree. _____

13. "I'm ten," Edward said. _____

14. The child said that she knew the answer. _____

15. "Did you watch TV last night?" Vikram asked. _____

Colour in your score

Test 3 Common expressions

We use many **common expressions** in our language.
Sometimes they are a little hard to understand.

For example, we say that when you give away a secret you
let the cat out of the bag!

Choose the correct word to complete each common expression.

1. to have an _____ to grind   (anvil/axe)

2. to hit below the _____   (belt/neck)

3. to take the _____ by the horns   (bull/devil)

4. to put the _____ before the horse   (apple/cart)

5. to be sent to _____   (Cambridge/Coventry)

6. to sit on the _____   (wall/fence)

7. to play second _____   (fiddle/string)

8. to bury the _____   (hatchet/hammer)

9. to strike while the _____ is hot   (weather/iron)

10. to turn over a new _____   (penny/leaf)

11. to make a _____ out of a molehill   (meal/mountain)

12. to face the _____   (music/front)

13. to smell a _____   (rat/dustbin)

14. to blow your own _____   (horn/trumpet)

15. to get into hot _____   (air/water)

Colour in your score

Test 4 **Adverbs**

An **adverb** tells us **more about a verb**.
Many adverbs end with the suffix **ly**.

The man waited **patiently**.

Make each of these adjectives into adverbs ending in ly.
Take care with the spelling.

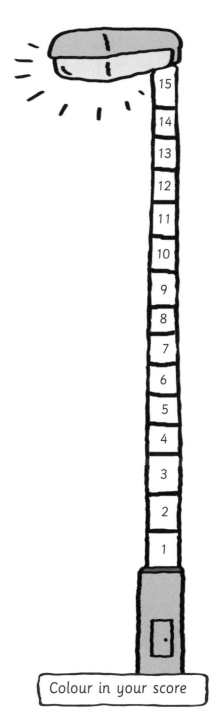

1. clever _____

2. poor _____

3. hungry _____

4. simple _____

5. grateful _____

6. lucky _____

7. heavy _____

8. idle _____

9. patient _____

10. merry _____

11. equal _____

12. feeble _____

13. fatal _____

14. loyal _____

15. lazy _____

Colour in your score

15
14
13
12
11
10
9
8
7
6
5
4
3
2
1

Test 5 Plurals

Rule 1: When a noun ends in **s**, **x**, **sh** or **ch**, we add **es** to make it plural.

Rule 2: When a noun ends in **f** (or **fe**), we usually change the **f** to **v** and add **es** to make it plural.

dish – dishes   leaf – leaves

Fill in the correct noun to complete each of these.

1. one calf, but two _____

2. one watch, but two _____

3. one loaf, but two _____

4. one brush, but two _____

5. one fox, but two _____

6. one shelf, but two _____

7. one wife, but two _____

8. one boss, but two _____

9. one _____, but two knives

10. one _____, but two boxes

11. one _____, but two wolves

12. one _____, but two glasses

13. one _____, but two branches

14. one _____, but two halves

15. one _____, but two wishes

Colour in your score

Test 6 Joining sentences

Two sentences may often be made into one sentence by using a **conjunction** (a **joining** word).

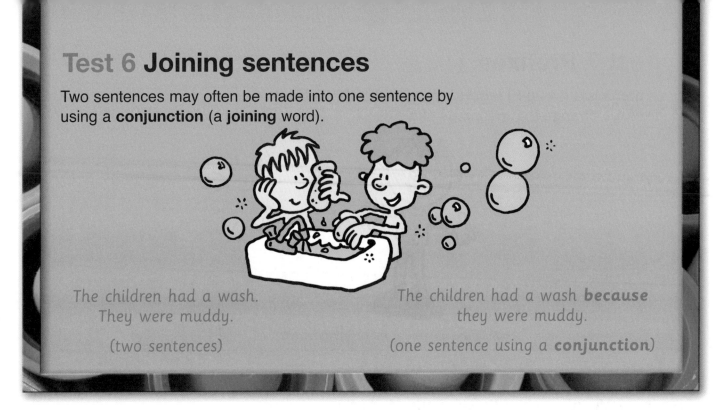

The children had a wash.
They were muddy.

(two sentences)

The children had a wash **because**
they were muddy.

(one sentence using a **conjunction**)

Underline the conjunction in each sentence.

1. John is a good swimmer but he is no good at drawing.

2. I like apples because they are sweet.

3. I saved my money so I could buy a toy.

4. I stayed out until it was dark.

5. I turned off the TV because I wanted to read.

6. It got too hot so I had a swim.

7. I was happy when I won the race.

8. I stopped at the kerb before I crossed the road.

9. My uncle gives me a present whenever he comes.

10. It started to rain after we went indoors.

11. I ran home so I could have my tea.

12. I got low marks although I tried hard.

13. Winter is nice but summer is better.

14. The leaves began to fall because it was autumn.

15. We watch TV when we get home.

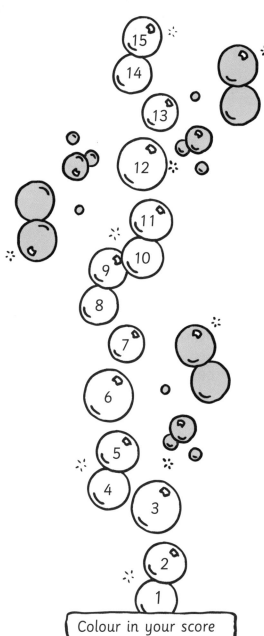

Colour in your score

Test 7 **Prefixes**

A **prefix** is a **group of letters** that go **in front** of a word.
Prefixes **change the meanings** of words.

visible   **in**visible

Take the prefix off each of these words. Write the
root word you are left with.

1. impatient   _____

2. irresponsible   _____

3. illegal   _____

4. incapable   _____

5. postcode   _____

6. recall   _____

7. triangle   _____

8. deport   _____

9. beside   _____

10. encircle   _____

11. exchange   _____

12. interact   _____

13. midnight   _____

14. nonsense   _____

15. overbalance   _____

Colour in your score

38

Test 8 Auxiliary verbs

Sometimes a verb needs a **helper** (or **auxiliary**) verb to help it make sense.

*Some children **were** climbing the tree.*

Choose the best auxiliary verb to complete each sentence.

1. Tom _____ looking in the shop window.   (is/are)

2. The girls _____ playing netball.   (is/are)

3. A car _____ speeding down the road.   (was/were)

4. The toads _____ croaking loudly.   (was/were)

5. I _____ going home.   (am/are)

6. We _____ approaching London.   (am/are)

7. I _____ whistle.   (can/has)

8. I _____ like to go if possible.   (would/could)

9. _____ you think you can run that fast?   (Do/Does)

10. Why _____ the sun set?   (do/does)

11. We _____ sail tomorrow.   (are/will)

12. What _____ the robber steal?   (did/do)

13. Next week I _____ going to the seaside.   (am/will)

14. Ben _____ not score a goal.   (do/did)

15. I _____ been to Coventry.   (has/have)

15

14

13

12

11

10

9

8

7

6

5

4

3

2

1

Colour in your score

Test 9 Suffixes

A **suffix** is a **group of letters** that can be added to the **end** of a word to **change its meaning** or the **way it is used**.

When we perform something we give a performance.

perform – perform**ance**

Match up the pairs of words with the same suffixes.

1.	treatment	collection
2.	assistant	disturbance
3.	action	punishment
4.	artist	interference
5.	appearance	attendant
6.	arrival	pressure
7.	justice	cyclist
8.	confidence	approval
9.	marriage	wisdom
10.	pleasure	service
11.	darkness	visitor
12.	childhood	blindness
13.	conductor	carriage
14.	discovery	parenthood
15.	kingdom	bakery

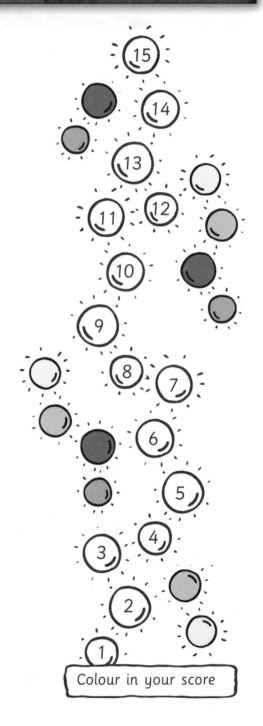

Colour in your score

Test 10 Verb tenses

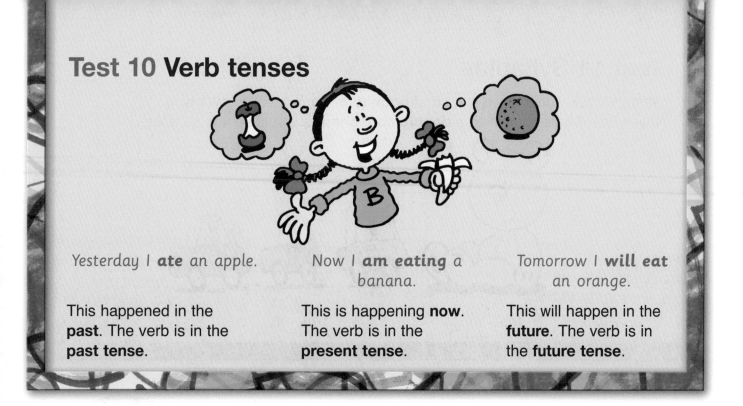

Yesterday I **ate** an apple.

This happened in the **past**. The verb is in the **past tense**.

Now I **am eating** a banana.

This is happening **now**. The verb is in the **present tense**.

Tomorrow I **will eat** an orange.

This will happen in the **future**. The verb is in the **future tense**.

Write what the tense of the verb is in each sentence.

1. Yesterday I fell over. _____

2. In the future we will travel in spaceships. _____

3. I am swimming in the lake. _____

4. Some birds are singing outside my window. _____

5. Tomorrow it will be my birthday. _____

6. In 1666 there was a great fire in London. _____

7. Laura drank a cup of tea. _____

8. Mr Shaw is mowing the lawn. _____

9. Will Scott win the cup? _____

10. Who is driving that car? _____

11. The man chopped down the tree. _____

12. I am going on a plane tomorrow. _____

13. Will it be sunny in the morning? _____

14. Last night I snored in bed. _____

15. Sarah is having a bath. _____

15
14
13
12
11
10
9
8
7
6
5
4
3
2
1

Colour in your score

Test 11 Syllables

We can break words down into **smaller units of sound**, called **syllables**.
Notice how words containing a **double consonant** are split up into syllables.

ted - dy   traf - fic

Split these words into two syllables.

1. barrow   _____ bar - row _____

2. berry   _____

3. pillow   _____

4. dinner   _____

5. rabbit   _____

6. sadder   _____

7. muffle   _____

8. wriggle   _____

9. slimming   _____

10. puppet   _____

11. assist   _____

12. batted   _____

13. dazzle   _____

14. cabbage   _____

15. office   _____

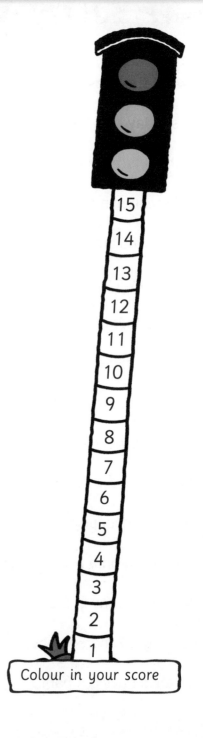

15
14
13
12
11
10
9
8
7
6
5
4
3
2
1

Colour in your score

Test 12 Common letter strings

Some words with the **same letter strings** are pronounced **differently**.

There are **mice** in the **office**.

Underline the odd word out in each set.

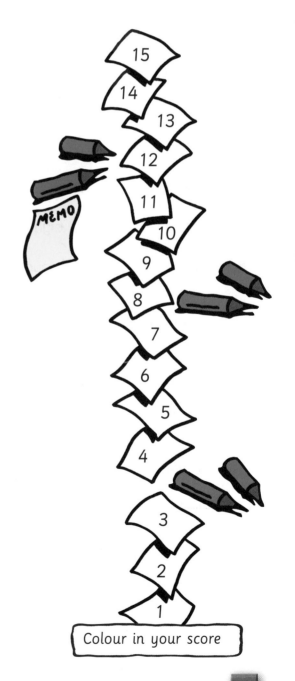

1. paddle   saddle   waddle

2. ball   call   shall

3. starter   quarter   charter

4. meat   beat   great

5. wear   near   year

6. here   there   where

7. what   chat   that

8. mice   nice   office

9. stamp   camp   swamp

10. shine   fine   engine

11. flower   lower   slower

12. home   some   dome

13. good   wood   flood

14. rose   nose   lose

15. touch   couch   pouch

Colour in your score

43

Test 13 Subject/verb agreement

The **subject** and **verb** in each sentence must **agree** with each other.

The hens **were** clucking.

Choose the correct form of the verb to agree with the subject in each sentence.

1. We _____ eating our dinner.   (was/were)

2. We _____ it last week.   (done/did)

3. The boy _____ making a model.   (is/are)

4. The children _____ shouting.   (is/are)

5. A spider _____ eight legs.   (has/have)

6. Snakes _____ through grass.   (slide/slides)

7. Ben _____ to wear jeans.   (like/likes)

8. History _____ my favourite subject.   (is/are)

9. I _____ my dinner.   (want/wants)

10. _____ you at home last night?   (Was/Were)

11. The price of the toy _____ too high.   (is/are)

12. Children _____ to school every day.   (go/goes)

13. Each of the apples _____ bad.   (is/are)

14. Fish and chips _____ a popular meal.   (is/are)

15. The number of cars _____ increasing.   (is/are)

Colour in your score

44

Test 14 Onomatopoeia

Onomatopoeia is when the **sound** of the word is **similar** to the **sound** of the thing it describes.

a clock **ticks**

Choose the word which best describes each sound.

1. the _____ of a bell   (clang/rattle)

2. the _____ of a trumpet   (beep/blare)

3. the _____ of raindrops   (patter/crunch)

4. the _____ of leaves   (rumble/rustle)

5. the _____ of brakes   (swish/screech)

6. the _____ of a hinge   (creak/click)

7. the _____ of a siren   (howl/wail)

8. the _____ of steam   (hiss/shuffle)

9. the _____ of an engine   (clang/chug)

10. the _____ of coins   (chime/chink)

11. the _____ of a drum   (pop/beat)

12. the _____ of an explosion   (blast/ping)

13. the _____ of water down a drain   (giggle/gurgle)

14. the _____ of dishes   (chatter/clatter)

15. the _____ of the wind   (shifting/sighing)

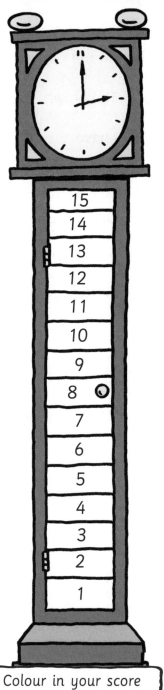

15
14
13
12
11
10
9
8
7
6
5
4
3
2
1

Colour in your score

Test 15 Homophones

Homophones are words that **sound the same** but are **spelt differently**.

*The boat with the torn **sail** was for **sale**.*

Choose the correct word to complete each sentence.

1. The brown _____ loved honey.   (bare/bear)

2. I have _____ a lot recently.   (groan/grown)

3. The _____ had large antlers.   (dear/deer)

4. Do _____ to me soon.   (write/right)

5. You need _____ to make cakes.   (flower/flour)

6. I paid my _____ and got off the bus.   (fare/fair)

7. The _____ was soft and ripe.   (pear/pair)

8. _____ is a type of meat.   (Stake/Steak)

9. We went for a _____ on a yacht.   (crews/cruise)

10. A _____ is found under a house.   (cellar/seller)

11. I had to _____ some cheese.   (grate/great)

12. An _____ is a small island.   (aisle/isle)

13. Another word for rough is _____.   (coarse/course)

14. Cornflakes is a breakfast _____.   (cereal/serial)

15. The soldier won a _____.   (medal/meddle)

Colour in your score

46

Test 16 **Soft** *c* **and** *g*

When the letter **c** is followed by **e**, **i** or **y**, it makes an **s** sound.

When the letter **g** is followed by **e**, **i** or **y**, it makes a **j** sound.

a prin**c**e with a **g**enie

Choose c or g to complete each of these words.

1. _____ity

2. stran_____e

3. _____entle

4. dan_____e

5. _____entre

6. pen_____e

7. _____iant

8. avera_____e

9. _____enerous

10. differen_____e

11. _____ertain

12. intelli_____ent

13. _____ircus

14. medi_____ine

15. ener_____y

Colour in your score

47

Test 17 Antonyms

An **antonym** is a word which has the **opposite** meaning.
Sometimes it can be made by adding a **prefix**.

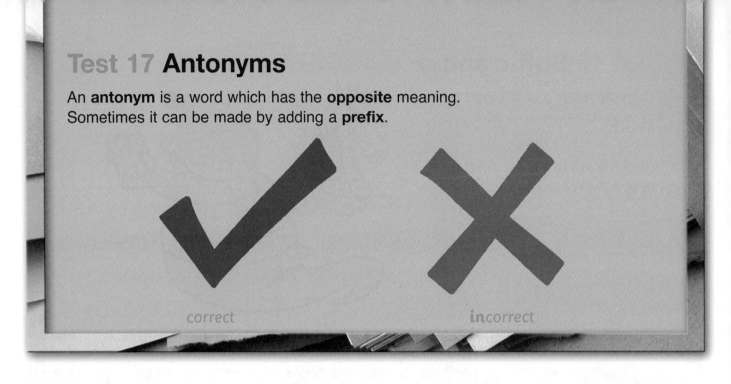

correct   **in**correct

Choose the correct prefix to give each word the opposite meaning.

1. _____safe   (un/dis)

2. _____behave   (im/mis)

3. _____obey   (un/dis)

4. _____selfish   (non/un)

5. _____patient   (in/im)

6. _____sane   (in/im)

7. _____sense   (un/non)

8. _____polite   (un/im)

9. _____regular   (il/ir)

10. _____logical   (il/ir)

11. _____noble   (il/ig)

12. _____pure   (in/im)

13. _____lock   (in/un)

14. _____loyal   (dis/mis)

15. _____normal   (ab/un)

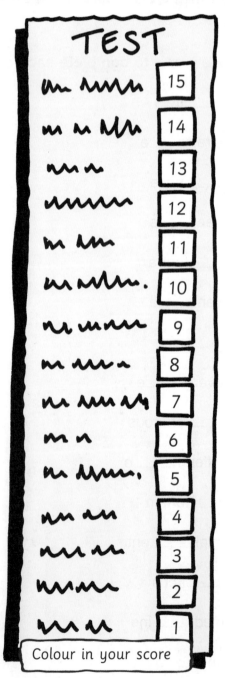

TEST

15
14
13
12
11
10
9
8
7
6
5
4
3
2
1

Colour in your score

48

Test 18 Doubling the consonant

When a verb ends with a **single consonant** preceded by a **short vowel**, we have to **double the consonant** before adding the suffix **ing** or **ed**.

rob ⟶ robbing ⟶ robbed

Add the suffix ing to these verbs.

1. tap _____

2. jog _____

3. hug _____

4. ban _____

5. begin _____

Add the suffix ed to these verbs.

6. nod _____

7. pop _____

8. wag _____

9. chat _____

10. travel _____

Take the suffix off the verb. Write the root verb you are left with.

11. shopping _____

12. mugged _____

13. ripped _____

14. stopping _____

15. grabbed _____

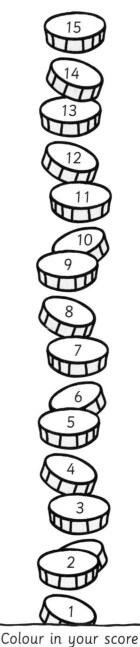

Colour in your score

49

Test 19 Making it clear

Sometimes the meanings of words can be **ambiguous** (unclear). We have to use the context of the sentence to work them out.

An elephant lifts its trunk.

<u>Underline</u> the meaning of the word in bold in each sentence.

1. My **trainer** was muddy.   (someone who coaches/you wear it on your foot)

2. I wore my **glasses**.   (you drink from them/you wear them to help you see)

3. The **bat** flew near me.   (you hit a ball with it/a mouse-like flying creature)

4. There was a **tap** on the door.   (you turn it on/someone knocking)

5. I looked at my **palm**.   (a type of tree/part of your hand)

6. The man lit his **pipe**.   (a tube water goes through/something you smoke)

7. There's a **fork** in the road.   (you eat with it/where a road divides into two)

8. The **bark** was brown.   (the sound a dog makes/you find it on tree trunks)

9. I put a case in the **boot**.   (part of a car/something you wear on your foot)

10. I bit my **nail**.   (you hit it with a hammer/part of a finger)

11. I played in the **match**.   (a game/used for lighting fires)

12. The sheep was in a **pen**.   (something to write with/an enclosure for animals)

13. The squirrel ate a **nut**.   (a metal bolt/it grows on trees)

14. There was a lot of **junk**.   (a Chinese ship/rubbish)

15. I ate a **date**.   (a type of fruit/a specific time)

15
14
13
12
11
10
9
8
7
6
5
4
3
2
1

Colour in your score

Test 20 Standard English

Standard English is the kind of language used in education, government and business.

Me and Sarah have been shopping. [X]

This is not grammatically correct.

Sarah and I have been shopping.

This is how it is written in Standard English.

Correct the underlined word in each of these sentences.

1. I saw the man ~~what~~ did it.   who   _____who_____

2. We didn't have <u>no</u> money.   _____

3. He <u>done</u> it yesterday.   _____

4. They could <u>of</u> done it easily.   _____

5. I <u>ain't</u> going.   _____

6. The man didn't say <u>nothing</u>.   _____

7. We <u>seen</u> the cat up the tree.   _____

8. The books <u>wasn't</u> in my desk.   _____

9. Do you <u>wanna</u> sweet?   _____

10. All of the children <u>was</u> dirty.   _____

11. He should have <u>took</u> more notice.   _____

12. He doesn't come here <u>no</u> more.   _____

13. Who has taken <u>me</u> socks?   _____

14. That's <u>real</u> terrible.   _____

15. I don't want <u>no</u> crisps   _____

Colour in your score

51

Test 21 Unstressed vowels

When we say some words it is **hard to hear** some of the vowels.
These are called **unstressed vowels**.

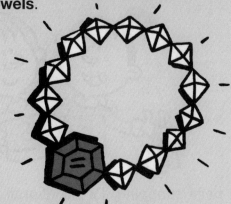

a diamond necklace

Fill in the missing unstressed vowel in each word.

1. usu____l

2. capt____in

3. veg____table

4. cam____ra

5. int____rest

6. libr____ry

7. temp____rature

8. diff____rent

9. bus____ness

10. secr____tary

11. valu____ble

12. parl____ament

13. hist____ry

14. sign____ture

15. nurs____ry

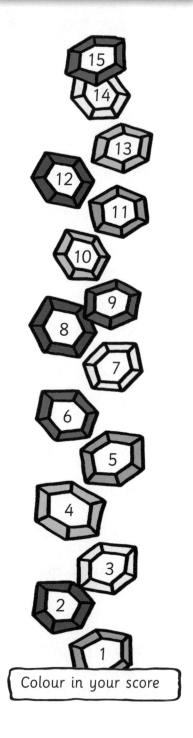

Colour in your score

52

Test 22 **Verbs ending with** *e*

When a verb ends with a **magic e**, we usually drop the **e** before we add
the suffix **ing** or **ed**.

bake → baking → baked

Yesterday I baked a cake.   Today I am baking some bread.

Add the suffix ing to these verbs.

1. rule _____

2. mope _____

3. dine _____

4. gape _____

5. bite _____

Add the suffix ed to these verbs.

6. rake _____

7. chime _____

8. hope _____

9. use _____

10. choke _____

**Take the suffix off these verbs. Write the root verb you
are left with.**

11. excusing _____

12. sloping _____

13. shining _____

14. forgiving _____

15. mistaking _____

Colour in your score

Test 23 Double negatives

This baby hasn't got no teeth. [X]

This sentence contains a **double negative**.

This baby hasn't got any teeth.

This sentence is written **correctly**.

Change these sentences to make them correct.

                       any

1. There aren't ~~no~~ sweets left.   _____any_____

2. I didn't go ~~nowhere~~ yesterday.   _____

3. I haven't ~~never~~ been to Spain.   _____

4. The boy said he didn't see ~~nobody~~.   _____

5. The car wasn't ~~nowhere~~ near the accident.   _____

6. I don't want ~~no~~ trouble.   _____

7. I can't find the book ~~nowhere~~.   _____

8. There isn't ~~no~~ point in arguing.   _____

9. The bike hasn't got ~~no~~ tyres.   _____

10. I didn't tell ~~no-one~~.   _____

11. I didn't say ~~nothing~~.   _____

12. I haven't ~~never~~ tasted mangoes.   _____

13. The thief wasn't ~~nowhere~~ to be seen.   _____

14. I didn't do ~~nothing~~ wrong.   _____

15. I haven't got ~~no~~ money.   _____

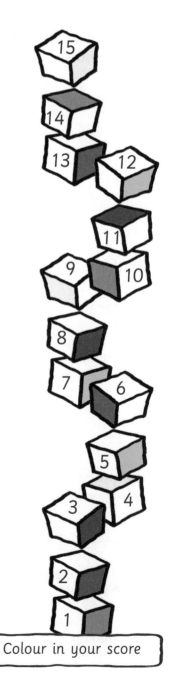

Colour in your score

54

Test 24 Sentences and phrases

The girl watched TV with her friend.

with her friend

A **sentence** contains a **verb**.
It **makes sense** on its own.

A **phrase** does **not** contain a verb.
It does **not** make sense on its own.

Write whether each of these is a sentence or a phrase.

1. A rabbit scampers. _____

2. in the morning _____

3. green and black _____

4. Yesterday Geeta passed her test. _____

5. I did my homework when I got home. _____

6. with neat handwriting _____

7. The car was left in the garage. _____

8. until Tuesday _____

9. My foot got stuck in the mud. _____

10. through the woods _____

11. because of the noise _____

12. The robber stole the jewels. _____

13. Some sparrows were looking for worms. _____

14. a loud banging noise _____

15. The rain fell heavily during the night. _____

15 14 13 12 11 10 9 8 7 6 5 4 3 2 1

Colour in your score

Test 25 Clauses

A **clause** is a **group of words** which can be used as a **whole sentence** or as **part of a sentence**. A clause must contain a **verb** and a **subject**.

Tom kicked the ball.
subject   verb

This is a **one-clause** sentence.

Underline the subject of each of these one-clause sentences.

1. Anna ate an apple.   (Anna/apple)

2. The farmer ploughed the field.   (farmer/field)

3. The chicken laid an egg.   (chicken/egg)

4. Bees live in hives.   (bees/hives)

5. Out of the door came Sam.   (door/Sam)

6. Through the wood came the dragon.   (wood/dragon)

7. We saw a dog in the park.   (we/dog)

8. The brave knight fell off the horse.   (knight/horse)

9. I wrote a long story.   (I/story)

10. The alien spoke a strange alien language.   (alien/language)

11. Suddenly a frog hopped past me.   (frog/me)

12. Rob likes sweets.   (Rob/sweets)

13. After the goal the crowd roared.   (goal/crowd)

14. Rockets fly in space.   (rockets/space)

15. In came the clowns with funny hats.   (clowns/hats)

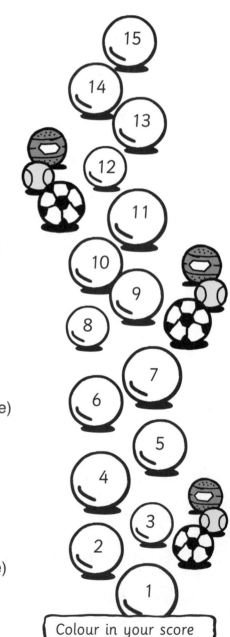

Colour in your score

Test 26 Prepositions

A **preposition** tells us the **position** of one thing in relation to another.

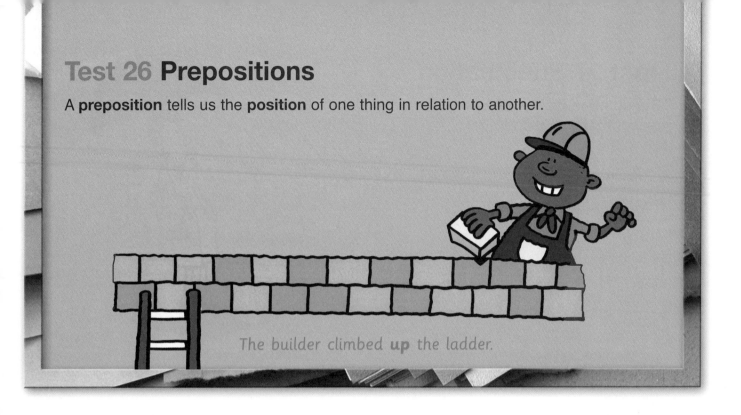

The builder climbed **up** the ladder.

Choose the best preposition to complete each sentence.

1. We stared _____ the strange sight. (by/at)

2. The fox walked _____ the woods. (through/beyond)

3. A tree was blown down _____ the storm. (during/until)

4. The man ran away _____ the fire. (off/from)

5. The dog jumped _____ the wall. (of/over)

6. I dropped a coin _____ the well. (before/down)

7. Don't mess about _____ electricity. (with/among)

8. I was thrilled _____ my present. (to/with)

9. The swimmer dived _____ the pool. (in/into)

10. The parade drove _____ the crowds. (against/past)

11. The train went _____ the bridge. (up/under)

12. Emma hid _____ a tree. (down/behind)

13. Tom stood _____ Sam and Ben. (through/between)

14. I pushed _____ the closed door. (against/for)

15. I fell _____ the wall. (up/off)

15
14
13
12
11
10
9
8
7
6
5
4
3
2
1

Colour in your score

Test 27 Punctuation

Punctuation marks help the
reader make sense of a text.

Mr Smith said what a nasty day ☒

This is not punctuated.

Mr Smith said, "What a nasty day!" ☑

This is punctuated. It is easier to read.

Fill in the missing punctuation mark in each sentence.

1. The sun went behind a cloud___

2. The man asked___ "Is it a nice day?"

3. What is the capital of Mexico___

4. It's not fair___

5. I___ve tried very hard.

6. "My dog is called Spot,___ Anna said.

7. After a while___ the queen appeared.

8. I saw a car, a bus___ a lorry and a bike.

9. The man said, ___Come with me."

10. "Pass the salt, Ben___" Mrs Jones said.

11. Yes___ it is my coat.

12. Don___t talk while you are eating.

13. Curry was Edward___s favourite food.

14. The girl shrieked, "I'm drowning___"

15. The car, a red sports car___ raced past.

15
14
13
12
11
10
9
8
7
6
5
4
3
2
1

Colour in your score

Test 28 Apostrophes for possession

We use **apostrophes** to show who or what something **belongs to**.

the man's hat

(the hat belonging to the man)

We add **'s** when there is only **one** owner.

the squirrels' nuts

(the nuts belonging to the squirrels)

We usually add **'** **after the s** if there is **more than one** owner.

Rewrite each phrase. Use the apostrophe correctly.

1. the apple belonging to the girl _____

2. the bike belonging to the boy _____

3. the car belonging to the doctor _____

4. the tools belonging to the builder _____

5. the hutch belonging to the rabbits _____

6. the purse belonging to Anna _____

7. the hats belonging to the soldiers _____

8. the lead belonging to the dog _____

9. the bags belonging to the ladies _____

10. the rocket belonging to the aliens _____

11. the house belonging to Mrs Shaw _____

12. the ship belonging to the sailors _____

13. the egg belonging to the bird _____

14. the toys belonging to the babies _____

15. the shell belonging to the snail _____

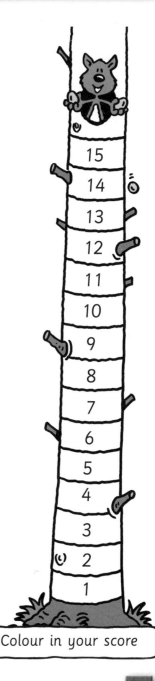

15
14
13
12
11
10
9
8
7
6
5
4
3
2
1

Colour in your score

Test 29 Making new words

We can sometimes **modify** a **root word** and turn it into a different **class of word**.

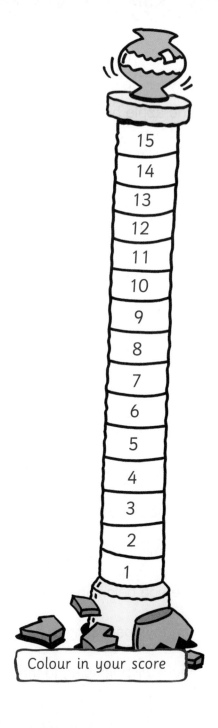

We can change some nouns into adjectives.

accident (a noun) – **accidental** (an adjective)

Match up the adjectives which come from each noun.

1. fashion	criminal	
2. fool	responsible	
3. giant	foolish	
4. crime	heroic	
5. danger	fashionable	
6. expense	comfortable	
7. hero	childish	
8. fable	merciful	
9. child	volcanic	
10. friend	gigantic	
11. mercy	woollen	
12. response	expensive	
13. comfort	fabulous	
14. volcano	friendly	
15. wool	dangerous	

Colour in your score

Test 30 Connecting clauses together

We sometimes use a **conjunction** (a **joining** word) to join two clauses together.

I eat lots of apples **because** they are so nice.

Choose the best conjunction to join the two clauses together.

1. I like climbing trees _____ I can hide.   (so/but)

2. I got angry _____ my friend upset me.   (if/when)

3. We go swimming _____ we can.   (and/whenever)

4. I went to bed _____ I ate my dinner.   (after/and)

5. I did it _____ I didn't want to.   (so/although)

6. I washed quickly _____ I was going out.   (because/when)

7. I read a book _____ I had tea.   (but/before)

8. Tom likes Kerry _____ Kerry doesn't like Tom.   (and/but)

9. I could not go out _____ I finished my spellings. (until/because)

10. I get annoyed _____ my sister pushes me.   (whenever/so)

11. I like swimming _____ it is good for me.   (because/after)

12. It got dark _____ I went home.   (so/but)

13. Ben likes football _____ enjoys playing cards.   (when/and)

14. Don't cross _____ the road is clear.   (if/until)

15. I would go _____ I was allowed to.   (so/if)

15
14
13
12
11
10
9
8
7
6
5
4
3
2
1

Colour in your score

61

ANSWERS

Page 2
I Common nouns are: coat, darkness, night, lion, school, house, bus.
Abstract nouns are: hatred, fear, jealousy, height, knowledge, expertise, joy.

II Many answers are possible.

Page 3
I
a patches   e pens
b toys   f dishes
c worries   g cities
d tries   h cakes

II
a hats   f buses
b parties   g trees
c bushes   h cries
d boxes   i books
e lorries   j puppies

Page 4
I
a pasta   h viola
b cobra   i risotto
c piano   j emu
d chapatti   k pizza
e gnu   l zebra
f cello   m camera
g tuba   n area

II
a zoos   f heroes
b radios   g dominoes
c echoes   h discos
d solos   i yo yos
e kimonos   j cuckoos

Page 5
I Active verbs are: a, b, d, f, i
Passive verbs are: c, e, g, h, j

II Many answers are possible.

Page 6
I
a play   d gobble   g are
b nibble   e fly   h needs
c swims   f grow

II
a chases   d is   g chase
b deliver   e eat   h are
c eats   f delivers

Page 7
I
a <u>It was hot</u>, so we had a cold drink.
b <u>My birthday is in October</u>, just before Hallowe'en.
c On Friday, <u>we are going on holiday</u>.
d Because it was so dark, <u>we took a torch</u>.
e <u>We flew to Greece</u>, on an aeroplane.
f <u>Susie is my best friend</u>, although I haven't known her very long.
g <u>The window got broken</u>, but it was an accident.
h <u>The shop was shut</u>, so we couldn't buy any sweets.

II
a <u>It was raining hard</u>, so I took an umbrella.
b <u>The bus was late</u>, so we had to walk.
c Because it was Saturday, <u>we could play football all day</u>.
d <u>Max has chickenpox</u>, so he has to stay at home.
e <u>I play the guitar</u>, although I'm <u>not very good.</u>
f <u>Mum lost her keys</u>, so we had to call a locksmith.
g <u>Dad drank all the tea</u>, so he had to buy some more.
h <u>The television broke down</u>, so I read my book.

Page 8
I
a boring, boredom
b lightning, delight
c impress, depression
d machinist, machinery
e breakfast, breakable
f operation, cooperate
g relative, relation
h building, rebuild

II Many answers are possible, but your child's answers may include:
a activity   action
b mistake   retake
c electrocute   electrify
d signal   signature
e reclaim   proclaim
f publication   publicity
g recover   discover
h children   childhood

Page 9
I
a peaceful   e circuits
b decide   f fearful
c city   g decimals
d careful   h hopeful

II
a cinema   e mouthful
b colourful   f decision
c harmful   g graceful
d circus   h circle

Page 10
I
a autograph
b circumference
c bifocals
d telephoto
e transparent
f bilingual
g circumstance
h transplant
i autobiography
j telegraph

II
a telephone   e bilingual
b bicycle   f automobile
c automatic   g television
d translate   h transfer

Page 11
I
a hot   e brave
b empty   f old
c angry   g exhausted
d wild   h broke

II Many answers are possible.

Page 12
I
a not acceptable
b feeling unwell
c very similar
d absolutely thrilled
e a great person to have around
f just like a parent
g raining very hard
h happens very rarely

II Many answers are possible.

Page 13
I
a 'Do you want to come back to my house after school?' asked Jamie.
b 'That would be great,' replied Sasha. 'I'll have to check with my mum though.'
c 'OK. If she says yes we could play with my new computer game.'
d 'I'll go and ask her now,' said Sasha. 'See you in a minute.'

II Exact wording may vary.
'Have you done your homework?' asked Dad.
'Not all of it,' replied John.
Dad said, 'You'll have to do the rest after tea.'
'But I'm supposed to be playing football with Stephen,' complained John.
'Well, Stephen will just have to wait while you finish your homework,' replied Dad.

Page 14
I
a proudly   e gloomily
b timidly   f crossly
c rudely   g sleepily
d confidently   h sulkily

II Many answers are possible.

Page 15
I Many answers are possible.

II Many answers are possible.

Page 16
I
a serial   f beech
b aloud   g steel
c board   h tale
d waste   i leek
e him   j weak

II We took our **fair** (fare) and went to **bye** (buy) a ticket for the boat trip. The **son** (sun) shone brightly as our boat docked at the (quay) **key**. A sailor with blonde (hair) **hare through** (threw) a long **peace** (piece) of rope to another sailor standing by us.
He **tide** (tied) it in a huge **not** (knot) to secure the boat. When the **mane** (main) gangplank appeared the passengers began to (board) **bored** the boat. We couldn't **weight** (wait) to set off!

Page 17

I
a politician e education
b confusion f possession
c direction g optician
d discussion h transfusion

II
a cian c ssion
b sion d tion

Page 18

I
a early f wide
b new g unhappy
c dull h short
d clean i slow
e ungrateful j disapprove

II Several answers are possible so exact answers may vary. Goldilocks found the bears' cottage in the woods and went inside. She tried the porridge. The **big** bear's porridge was too **hot**. The little bear's porridge was too cold. She sat down. The **big** bear's chair was too **high**. The small bear's chair was too low. She tried their beds. The **big** bear's bed was too hard. The tiny bear's bed was too soft. Goldilocks fell **asleep**, but when the bears returned she was wide awake immediately. The bears chased Goldilocks away. She ran **fast** and they were too slow to catch her.

Page 19

I
a whispers e crash
b crunch f squelched
c squealed g dripped
d clanged h splashed

II Several answers are possible.

Page 20

I
a She is unpredictable.
b She is a good person.
c He is difficult to understand.
d We have a family secret.
e We are treating ourselves.
f She can't be trusted.
g He is annoying.
h She is trustworthy.

II Exact answers may vary.
a There will be one bad person in every group.
b He is strong and dependable.
c Something good comes from every problem.
d She may represent a hidden danger.
e He is clumsy and out of control.
f You're a real help.

Page 21

I The personal pronouns are:
a She d We g you
b They e me h them
c us f I

II
a Susie is my friend and she lives next door.
b The boys jumped on their bikes, because they didn't want to be late.
c Sam and I bought some sweets and we had a bag each.
d Jo and I went to the cinema and we bought some popcorn.
e Mum and Dad left us with Gran last night, so they could go out.
f Dad collects my sisters from school and then takes them to Brownies.

Page 22

I
a My friend, who is called Chris, is coming to tea.
b Tomorrow, after lunch, we are going to the zoo.
c My brother, who is older than me, is great at football.
d Yesterday, because it was hot, we went to the beach.
e Our teacher, Mrs Brooks, marked our books.
f The new cinema, in town, has five screens.
g Donuts, with holes in, are my favourite cakes.
h A letter, with American stamps, came for me today.

II
a My Uncle, who is from Australia, is coming to visit.
b Tomorrow, after school, we are going bowling.
c The train, which was late, was crowded **or** The train, which was crowded, was late.
d The dog, called Patch, chased its tail.
e The new coat, which is blue, is really warm.
f Next week, on Tuesday, we are going on holiday.

Page 23

I The narrator is the shoemaker.

II Many answers are possible.

Page 24

I macaroni, mango, biryani, risotto, chapatti, tortilla, chow mein, moussaka.

II
a France d China
b Italy e India
c Australia
Sentences using the words will vary.

Page 25

I
a all hallows' eve
b personal computer
c heavy goods vehicle
d public house
e salt and vinegar
f aeroplane
g hire purchase
h omnibus

II
a television
b photograph
c physical education
d fish and chips
e bicycle
f very important person
g member of parliament
h refrigerator
i United Kingdom

Page 26

I The prepositions are:
a over d to, after g between
b through e under h on
c from f into

II Exact answers may vary, but appropriate prepositions are:
a behind d into g on
b over e on h along
c in f into

Page 27

I
a A dog's tail.
b The women's shopping.
c A girl's books.
d Two boys' socks.
e Four horses' stables.
f The people's cheers.
g A cook's apron.
h A cat's kittens.

II
a The cows' fields.
b The teachers' pupils.
c The children's rooms.
d The dogs' kennels.
e The hens' eggs.
f The bakers' cakes.
g The men's shoes.
h The cars' tyres.

Page 28

I Many answers are possible.

II Many answers are possible.

Page 29

I
a The cat licked its paws.
b Ben wrote to his pen pal.
c Sarah drank her juice.
d The king sat on his throne.
e The bull charged across its field.
f The girls read their books.
g We watched our favourite film.
h They sang their song.

II
a her e its
b their f my
c his g their
d our h its

Page 30

I
a After all the hunting, we found the key.
b My favourite subject at school is geography.
c It was great on holiday!
d We tidied up, then got ready to go home.
e What time is it?
f Before school, we walked the dog.

II Last September, we moved house. Our new house is brilliant! I remember when Mum said we were going to move. 'Why?' I asked. She said, 'Our new house will have more space and a bigger garden.' She was right. Now we have lots of space and my best friend, who is called Julie, lives next door.

Page 31

I
a general k boundary
b separate l conservatory
c prosperous m generous
d interested n history
e memorable o dangerous
f offering p mystery
g difference q boisterous
h library r christening
i fastener s listening
j desperate t stationery

II
a frightening f conference
b business g reference
c factory h voluntary
d explanatory i happening
e category j literacy

Page 32
1. aid
2. crafty
3. tiny
4. prevent
5. foe
6. complain
7. gather
8. cure
9. within
10. hard
11. ill
12. wide
13. fast
14. miserable
15. crazy

Page 33
1. direct
2. reported
3. reported
4. direct
5. direct
6. reported
7. direct
8. reported
9. reported
10. direct
11. direct
12. reported
13. direct
14. reported
15. direct

Page 34
1. axe
2. belt
3. bull
4. cart
5. Coventry
6. fence
7. fiddle
8. hatchet
9. iron
10. leaf
11. mountain
12. music
13. rat
14. trumpet
15. water

Page 35
1. cleverly
2. poorly
3. hungrily
4. simply
5. gratefully
6. luckily
7. heavily
8. idly
9. patiently
10. merrily
11. equally
12. feebly
13. fatally
14. loyally
15. lazily

Page 36
1. calves
2. watches
3. loaves
4. brushes
5. foxes
6. shelves
7. wives
8. bosses
9. knife
10. box
11. wolf
12. glass
13. branch
14. half
15. wish

Page 37
1. but
2. because
3. so
4. until
5. because
6. so
7. when
8. before
9. whenever
10. after
11. so
12. although
13. but
14. because
15. when

Page 38
1. patient
2. responsible
3. legal
4. capable
5. code
6. call
7. angle
8. port
9. side
10. circle
11. change
12. act
13. night
14. sense
15. balance

Page 39
1. is
2. are
3. was
4. were
5. am
6. are
7. can
8. would
9. Do
10. does
11. will
12. did
13. am
14. did
15. have

Page 40
1. punishment
2. attendant
3. collection
4. cyclist
5. disturbance
6. approval
7. service
8. interference
9. carriage
10. pressure
11. blindness
12. parenthood
13. visitor
14. bakery
15. wisdom

Page 41
1. past
2. future
3. present
4. present
5. future
6. past
7. past
8. present
9. future
10. present
11. past
12. future
13. future
14. past
15. present

Page 42
1. bar - row
2. ber - ry
3. pil - low
4. din - ner
5. rab - bit
6. sad - der
7. muf - fle
8. wrig - gle
9. slim - ming
10. pup - pet
11. as - sist
12. bat - ted
13. daz - zle
14. cab - bage
15. of - fice

Page 43
1. waddle
2. shall
3. quarter
4. great
5. wear
6. here
7. what
8. office
9. swamp
10. engine
11. flower
12. some
13. flood
14. lose
15. touch

Page 44
1. were
2. did
3. is
4. are
5. has
6. slide
7. likes
8. is
9. want
10. Were
11. is
12. go
13. is
14. is
15. is

Page 45
1. clang
2. blare
3. patter
4. rustle
5. screech
6. creak
7. wail
8. hiss
9. chug
10. chink
11. beat
12. blast
13. gurgle
14. clatter
15. sighing

Page 46
1. bear
2. grown
3. deer
4. write
5. flour
6. fare
7. pear
8. Steak
9. cruise
10. cellar
11. grate
12. isle
13. coarse
14. cereal
15. medal

Page 47
The missing letters are in **bold**.
1. **c**ity
2. **s**trange
3. **g**entle
4. **d**ance
5. **c**entre
6. **p**ence
7. **g**iant
8. avera**g**e
9. **g**enerous
10. differen**c**e
11. **c**ertain
12. intelli**g**ent
13. **c**ircus
14. medi**c**ine
15. ener**g**y

Page 48
The missing prefixes are in **bold**.
1. **un**safe
2. **mis**behave
3. **dis**obey
4. **un**selfish
5. **im**patient
6. **in**sane
7. **non**sense
8. **im**polite
9. **ir**regular
10. **il**logical
11. **ig**noble
12. **im**pure
13. **un**lock
14. **dis**loyal
15. **ab**normal